Emotional Intelligence

Linda Wasmer Andrews

Franklin Watts
A Division of Scholastic Inc.
New York • Toronto • London • Auckland • Sydney
Mexico City • New Delhi • Hong Kong
Danbury, Connecticut

Dedication

For Amanda and Tim,
an emotionally brilliant pair

Cover design by John Gibson.
Interior design by Kathleen Santini.
Photos pp. 60-61 by James Levin / Studio 10
Special thanks to our model, Joelle Hernandez

Library of Congress Cataloging-in-Publication Data

Andrews, Linda Wasmer.
    Emotional intelligence / Linda Wasmer Andrews.
        v. cm. — (Life balance)
Includes bibliographical references and index.
Contents: Dealing with feeling—Name that emotion!—Understanding yourself—Handling your emotions—Managing relations—Glossary—Further resources.
    ISBN 0-531-12335-9 (lib. bdg.)   0-531-16688-0 (pbk.)
    1. Emotional intelligence—Juvenile literature. [1. Emotional intelligence. 2. Emotions.] I. Title. II. Series.
    BF576.A53 2004
    152.4—dc22
                                2003019772

Table of Contents

Dealing With Feeling

Imagine this: Becca and Josh are best friends in the same history class. When the teacher hands back their essay tests in class, Becca has an A, and Josh has a D. After class, the friends walk to their lockers together. Josh complains loudly, "It's not fair! That teacher has it out for me. You have all the luck!"

Becca can't believe how unreasonable Josh is being. Apparently, her friend has forgotten that Becca stayed home to study while Josh went to the movies the night before the test. Before she knows what's happening, Becca can feel her heart start to pound and her breathing grow faster. What should Becca say?

A. "Grow up! You're such a little crybaby."

B. "Maybe we could study together next time."

C. "I can tell you're upset. I have to go to English class right now, but we can talk some more at lunch, okay?"

D. Becca should keep quiet and just ignore Josh's comment.

Answer A isn't going to help anything. Josh is already upset. If Becca comes back with an angry remark now, the two are probably going to end up in a big argument. Answer B is a good suggestion, but this may be the wrong time to make it. Josh seems too upset to think about things clearly right now. It might be better for Becca to wait until Josh has had a chance to calm down. Then the friends can discuss possible solutions to the problem, such as studying together.

Answer C may be a better choice. Josh isn't the only one upset here. If Becca is in tune with her own feelings, she probably realizes that she is getting angry, too. Surprisingly, many people have trouble recognizing anger in themselves. All of their lives, they may have been told, "Don't get mad!" "Stop yelling!" "Calm down!" Before long, they may have become very good at hiding signs of strong emotion from other people—so good that they even try to hide their feelings from themselves. As soon as a strong feeling such as anger starts bubbling up, many people try to push it back down and pretend it doesn't exist. Yet the feeling is still there, and it affects people physically and mentally.

In Becca's case, the pounding heart and fast breathing are clues to her anger. So are her thoughts about how unreasonable Josh is being. Chances are that both friends would have trouble discussing things calmly right now. It's smart for them to take a short time-out before they try to talk. This gives them a chance to deal with their own feelings first. Then they can use their feelings to guide what they do and say so that it helps, not hurts, their friendship.

Of course, it's important that the friends work things out eventually. That's why answer D is not a great choice. Instead of ignoring her anger, Becca needs to recognize it. Recognizing what emotion she's feeling gives her vital information, because anger is a signal that something is wrong. If Becca thinks about it, maybe she'll realize that she's really bugged because Josh never seems to give her credit for her hard work. The friends can talk about this problem later, when they're both calmer.

However, Becca might never have realized there even *was* a problem if she hadn't noticed her anger. First, she identified what she was feeling. Then, she used that information as a starting point for thinking through the situation and figuring out a good way of handling it. Finally, she let this thinking guide her actions. Whether she knew it or not, Becca was showing lots of emotional intelligence (EI for short).

"Anyone can become angry—that is easy. But to be angry at the right person, to the right degree, at the right time, for the right purpose, and in the right way—that is not easy."
—Aristotle (384–322 B.C.),
Greek philosopher

Why Emotional Intelligence Is Smart

Different people define EI in slightly different ways. In general, though, it refers to the ability to notice, understand, and manage your own emotions and those of others. This ability lets you use emotional information to guide your thoughts and actions in a helpful way. EI is similar to ordinary intelligence in that it involves using information in a way that helps you achieve your goals. With the kind of intelligence measured by school tests, however, you are working mainly with facts, words, and numbers. With EI, you are working with your knowledge of emotions.

Some people just seem to be particularly good at getting along with others and understanding their feelings. When we talk about these folks, we say things such as "She's great with people" or "It's almost like he can read my mind." Other people seem to be especially good at knowing what they want and going after it. When we talk about these people, we say things such as "She really knows her own mind" or "Once he has his mind set on something, nothing is going to stop him."

These are the kinds of people who are high in EI. Their ability to understand and use emotional information helps them do well at home, school, and work. Their ability to express themselves and influence others makes them natural leaders as well. EI seems to go hand in hand with success in many areas of life.

"Emotional intelligence counts more than IQ or expertise for determining who excels at a job—any job."
—Daniel Goleman, American author and psychologist

The good news is that EI seems to be largely learned. It continues to grow as you mature and learn from your experiences. This means that even if you aren't exactly an emotional genius now, you can improve your EI with a little practice. Why bother? EI can come in handy in all sorts of situations. For example:

- It can help you control your temper when you get angry.
- It can give you the motivation to go after your goals.
- It can help you tell when someone is lying to you.
- It can help you cope with bullies and other difficult people.
- Maybe most important, it can give you more insight into a really fascinating person—you!

Other Kinds of Smart

Everyone agrees that the ability to understand and manage emotions can come in very handy. Not everyone thinks it is a type of intelligence, however. Some scientists prefer to use the term *intelligence* only for the kind of mental ability that involves working with ideas, words, and numbers. These scientists say that other abilities may be nice talents to have, but that doesn't make them forms of intelligence.

However, many experts now hold a different view. They say that there is more than one way to be smart. These experts believe that intelligence can take several forms, all of which are equally valid. One of those forms involves being smart about emotions. Two of the leading thinkers in this field are Howard Gardner and Robert Sternberg.

Gardner, a professor of education at Harvard University, has suggested that there are eight different forms of intelligence. The two that are closely related to EI are highlighted in bold type below.

- **Interpersonal intelligence** — the ability to understand the feelings and goals of other people.
- **Intrapersonal intelligence** — the ability to understand your own feelings and goals.
- Linguistic intelligence — the ability to use words well.

- Logical-mathematical intelligence — the ability to think logically and use numbers well.
- Spatial intelligence — the ability to create mental images in order to solve problems.
- Musical intelligence — the ability to recognize and create musical pitches, tones, and rhythms.
- Bodily-kinesthetic intelligence — the ability to use the mind to coordinate the body's movements.
- Naturalist intelligence — the ability to recognize different plants and animals.

Sternberg, a psychologist at Yale University, has proposed that there are three parts to intelligence. The one that is closely related to EI is highlighted in bold type below.

- **Practical intelligence** — the ability to understand and solve real-life problems; it is similar to common sense or "street smarts."
- Analytical intelligence — the ability to analyze ideas, solve abstract problems, and make decisions.
- Creative intelligence — the ability to go beyond what is known to come up with new and interesting ideas.

The New Science of EI

EI is like breathing—it seems obvious that it's really important, but you probably don't think much about it. Instead, you just take it for granted. People have long recognized that understanding yourself and others is a useful skill. However, it is only recently that scientists have begun to systematically study EI.

The new science of EI is rooted in two older ideas: emotion and intelligence. An emotion is a mental feeling that comes up without conscious effort and leads to a state of arousal. Examples include anger, fear, joy, love, and hate. Emotional arousal, in turn, gives rise to the impulse to act. In fact, the word *emotion* comes from the Latin word *movere*, which means "to move." Acting on emotion without thinking first can lead to trouble, however. That's why people who are high in EI learn to assess their impulses and curb them if necessary. You may have an impulse to hit someone when you're angry, for example, but actually doing so wouldn't be very smart.

Intelligence refers to the ability to learn and then put that learning to good use. Many scientists today believe that EI is a type of intelligence, because it requires learning and using information. With ordinary intelligence, that information might involve ideas, words, or numbers. With EI, though, it involves emotions. Let's say you've just started class at a new school, and you want to make friends. At lunch, another student looks you straight in the eye and smiles at you. Based on your past learning, you think that this probably means the student is feeling friendly. You go up and introduce yourself. Before you know it, you've made a new friend thanks to using EI.

Two American psychologists named Peter Salovey and John Mayer first coined the term *EI* in 1990. Since then, they have continued to study the subject. They have even developed a test similar to the IQ tests that are used to measure ordinary intelligence. On regular IQ tests, however, people solve logic problems and answer questions that call for factual information or the use of words and numbers. On Salovey and Mayer's EI test, people do tasks such as identifying the emotion shown in a photograph of a face or choosing the emotion that a person would probably feel in a particular situation. Salovey and Mayer now believe that EI has four main parts.

- **Understanding emotion**—knowing about emotions and their meanings. For example, this includes being able to put a name to what you're feeling and knowing how to pick out the different feelings that make up mixed emotions.
- **Emotional perception**—being aware of emotions. For example, this includes noticing emotions in yourself

and being able to identify what other people are feeling based on clues such as their facial expressions.

- **Managing emotion**—handling emotions in a positive way. For example, this includes staying open to your emotions and using the information you gain to promote emotional and mental growth.
- **Emotional facilitation**—using emotions to improve thinking. For example, this includes using your emotions to shift your thinking in a helpful direction and improve your skill at making decisions.

At first, EI was a little-known idea. Then, in 1995, another American psychologist named Daniel Goleman published a best-selling book called *Emotional Intelligence*. In response, *Time* magazine ran a cover story about EI. The American Dialect Society picked "emotional intelligence" as one of the year's most useful new phrases. Suddenly, EI was a household word. Scientists and the public alike were drawn to the new concept.

Parts of a Whole

The whole idea of EI is so new that scientists are still trying to figure out exactly what it includes. Peter Salovey and John Mayer have developed a four-part theory of EI. Daniel Goleman has developed a slightly different five-part theory. Not surprisingly, though, the two theories have a lot in common. Here is how they compare.

Theories of EI

What It Is	What Salovey and Mayer Call It	What Goleman Calls It	Chapter in This Book About It
Knowing about emotions and their meanings	Understanding emotion	Knowing one's emotions	2
Being aware of your own emotions	Emotional perception	Knowing one's emotions	3
Handling your own emotions in a positive way	Managing emotion	Managing emotions	4
Using emotions to improve thinking	Emotional facilitation	Motivating oneself	4
Being aware of other people's emotions	Emotional perception	Recognizing emotions in others	5
Handling other people's emotions in a positive way	Managing emotion	Handling relationships	5

The Marshmallow Challenge

In his book, Goleman described a classic psychology study, which he nicknamed the "marshmallow challenge." The study started in the 1960s at a preschool on the campus of Stanford University. Researchers there offered four-year-olds a choice: If they waited until after the researcher had run an errand, they could have two marshmallows. If they couldn't wait, they could have a marshmallow right away, but only one.

The idea was to find out if four-year-olds would be able to resist the impulse to grab a marshmallow immediately. This kind of emotional self-control is at the heart of EI. Some of the children gave in to the impulse, but others were able to wait several minutes for the two-marshmallow reward. Years later, these same children were tracked down as teenagers. The researchers found big differences between those who had waited for the marshmallows and those who hadn't.

The children who had waited grew into teenagers who were less likely to go to pieces under stress. They also tended to be more skillful at dealing with people. These teens liked challenges and worked toward goals instead of giving up at the first sign of difficulty. They were generally confident and reliable. In high school, they were also better students, on average, than the other teens.

On the other hand, the children who had grabbed for the marshmallows had more trouble coping with stress as they grew older. They also tended to shy away from other people. These teens became frustrated quickly and lost their temper easily. As a result, they got into more than their share of arguments and fights.

Why did the children who had waited for a marshmallow have an easier time as they grew up? Most likely, it was because they had better emotional self-control. The ability to delay rewards and work toward long-term goals is critical for all kinds of life successes, from winning a sports contest to getting into a good college. It's also one of the most important benefits of EI. Even if you were the kind of kid who always grabbed for the marshmallow, though, you can learn to boost your EI now. This book will get you started.

Two

Name That
Emotion

Remember Becca and Josh, the bickering buddies from Chapter one? Let's imagine them in a new situation. This time, Becca suggests they go for a bike ride after school, but Josh says he has to mow the lawn. Later that afternoon, Becca is riding past the park when she sees Josh skateboarding there. Becca feels her heart begin racing and her legs start pedaling faster and faster. She tells herself that she doesn't mind, though.

The next day at school, Josh asks Becca if she wants to go for a bike ride that afternoon. All of a sudden, Becca is angry. "I have a life, you know!" she says. "I'm *busy* this afternoon." Josh is surprised. Why is

Becca acting this way toward him? Even Becca is caught off guard by her own reaction.

Josh snaps back. Before long, the two friends are yelling, and Becca has gone from angry to enraged. Finally, she says something really mean. Josh walks away, and Becca is left by herself, feeling guilty and confused.

Now let's rewrite the story so that it has a happier ending. When Becca sees Josh skateboarding, she realizes that she's angry as soon as she begins pedaling furiously. She understands that anger is a warning sign that something is wrong. Often, it means your feelings are hurt because you think someone has behaved unjustly toward you. In this case, Becca thinks that Josh may have lied because he didn't want to hang out with her. Becca is angry, but underneath that, she's also hurt.

At school the next day, Becca asks what happened. Josh explains that he finished mowing the lawn earlier than expected, so he went skateboarding for a while. Becca realizes she had jumped to the wrong conclusion the previous afternoon. The two friends make plans to ride bikes together after school. The moral of the story: Life is a smoother ride when you understand emotions and their meanings.

"But I Know When I'm Mad!"

Don't people just *know* when they're angry or their feelings are hurt? Not always. People often get confusing messages as they're growing up about how they're supposed to feel. They're told, "Don't get angry!" "Don't be a baby!" "Only sissies cry!" As a result, they may learn to ignore their own emotions. Like Becca in the first version of the story above, they may find themselves caught off guard by their reactions to feelings they hadn't even noticed they were having.

A century ago, an Austrian physician named Sigmund Freud revolutionized ideas about how the human mind works. Freud stressed that people often hide or disguise their true feelings, even from themselves. He used the term *repression* to describe the forcing of unpleasant feelings or painful memories from the conscious part of the mind to the unconscious. Today, it is widely believed that people often try to ignore emotions that they find awkward or unpleasant. The feelings are still there, though, and people can learn to become more aware of them with practice.

"There can be no knowledge without emotion. We may be aware of a truth, but until we have felt its force, it is not ours."
—Arnold Bennett (1867–1931),
British novelist

Some people just never learned to label their emotions correctly in the first place. This isn't something we are born knowing how to do. Instead, it's a skill that is mastered over time. As children get better at this skill, their vocabulary for describing emotions also grows larger and more precise.

By age two, many children can pick out "happy" faces from photographs, and some can also pick out "sad" and "mad" faces. By age five, most can also identify faces that are "surprised" and "scared." By sixth or seventh grade, many know that two emotions can blend and interact to produce a new feeling. For example, sadness and anger may combine to create depression. However, just as some children learn to read, draw, or play ball better than others, there are also differences in how well people master the ability to notice and name their emotions.

Mixed Emotions

When you mix the colors yellow and blue, you wind up with a whole new color: green. Likewise, when you mix emotions, you might wind up with a whole new feeling. Match the combinations on the left with the feelings they may create on the right.

1. surprise + fear = _____   *A. love*

2. disgust + fear = _____   *B. disappointment*

3. surprise + sadness = _____   *C. hatred*

4. joy + acceptance = _____   *D. shame*

5. disgust + anger = _____   *E. alarm*

Answers: (1) E, (2) D, (3) B, (4) A, (5) C

Fortunately, like other abilities, this one can be improved with conscious effort.

How Are You Feeling?

Emotions are inner feelings, but they often produce outer signs. By paying close attention to these signs, you can begin to understand the feelings behind them. The first step is to start noticing your arousal—the bodily changes that go along with emotional states. Different emotions lead to different levels of arousal.

Some emotions set off alarm bells in your brain. They tell your brain to prepare your body for quick action in response to a threat. For example, let's say you're walking down the sidewalk alone when you see three gang members headed your way. You view the gang members as a threat, and you feel afraid. At the same time, your brain tells your body to get ready in case you need to fight or run.

Your body draws on its fuel stores for a quick burst of energy. Your breathing speeds up. This supplies your body with the extra oxygen it needs to use the fuel for energy production. Your heart beats faster, too. This brings more blood containing fuel and oxygen to places where you need it, such as your muscles and brain. At the same time, your muscles tense up as you brace for action.

Fear and anger are emotions that lead to high arousal. This explains why you may feel like hitting someone when you're angry or like running out of the room when you're scared. On the other hand, sadness is an emotion that leads to low arousal. Instead of fighting or fleeing, you may feel more like quietly withdrawing into a shell when you're sad. Other emotions fall somewhere in between. For example, when you're irritated, you may feel a little snappish. When you're nervous, you may feel a little jittery. And when you're happy, you may feel like jumping for joy.

It would be very handy if Sign X always meant you were feeling Emotion Y. Unfortunately, life isn't that simple. The same bodily sign can mean different things in different situations. For example, crying usually goes along with sadness. However, people also cry from relief or even from great joy. There are no hard-and-fast rules, but there are some general guidelines. These are some of the bodily signs that often go along with specific emotions.

- joy—faster heartbeat, relaxed muscles, feeling warm, laughing, smiling
- fear—faster heartbeat, tense muscles, change in breathing, feeling cold, sweating
- anger—faster heartbeat, tense muscles, change in breathing, feeling hot, yelling

- sadness—faster heartbeat, tense muscles, feeling cold, crying, lump in throat

Some of these signs involve body temperature. You may never have given much thought before to the link between temperature and emotion. Chances are, however, you were at least dimly aware of the connection. Several common sayings in our language are based on this link.

- joy—"Their kindness warmed my heart."
- fear—"I was in a cold sweat."
- fear—"My blood ran cold."
- anger—"I was hot under the collar."

"People's feelings turn cool and warm; the ways of the world run hot and cold." —Chinese proverb

The bodily signs listed above are good rules of thumb. You have your own unique style of reacting to emotions, however. The best way to learn about it is to observe yourself. The next time you feel joyful, afraid, angry, or sad, ask yourself what bodily changes you notice. Later on, whenever you feel confused about your feelings, your bodily reactions can help you figure things out. For example, let's say the cute student who sits next to you in math class strikes up a conversation. Mostly, you feel very happy about this. However, you also notice that your palms are getting sweaty. From your past experience, you know this means that you're a little nervous, too. This information, in turn, tips you off: Now might be a great time to take a few deep, calming breaths.

Emotions vs. Moods

Emotions are like the weather. They are always changing in response to hourly and even minute-by-minute conditions. In contrast, moods are more like the climate of a region. They are wider-ranging and longer-lasting. For example, you're sure to feel a little sad, afraid, or angry now and then. At times, however, your blue, worried, or cranky feelings may last for hours or days. They start to color how you see almost everything in the world. The scientific name for this is dysphoria—an unpleasant mood. The opposite is euphoria—an overly keyed-up mood. Luckily, there is also a middle ground. The fancy term for this is euthymia— a mood that leads to mental peace and happiness.

Cooling Off and Calming Down

Life would be flat and boring without emotional ups and downs. That's the good side of emotional arousal. However, there is a bad side, too: When your arousal level gets too high, it can be hard to think clearly. You may be so distracted by your pounding heart or flip-flopping stomach that it's nearly impossible to sort out your thoughts. When you're very upset, you may need to cool off or calm down before doing anything else. Otherwise, you might make rash decisions that you later regret. These tips can help you bring your arousal back down to a cooler, calmer level.

Count to ten. This really works! Breathe slowly and deeply. Try to make your belly inflate like a balloon as you breathe in and flatten as you breathe out. Continue breathing in a slow, steady rhythm. Now, as you breathe in, say "One" to yourself. Then breathe out. As you breathe in the next time, say "Two." Then breathe out. Keep going until you reach ten. Check how you're feeling. Have your heart rate, breathing, and other bodily signs returned to normal? If not, repeat the process counting backward from ten to one.

Crack a joke. Sometimes a little humor can go a long way toward breaking the tension. Just be sure not to joke around at someone else's expense. Laugh at the situation, not at another person.

Give yourself a time-out. You've tried everything else, and you're still very upset. You feel an argument about to break out. It may be time to remove yourself from the situation for a few minutes. This gives you a chance to calm down and collect your thoughts. By then, you should be thinking clearly enough to talk things out calmly with the other person. Often, excusing yourself to go to the bathroom or get a drink of water is all the time you need. If you have to wait longer, set a

Feelings, From Angst to Zest

Once you're calm, it helps to talk about whatever you're feeling. Sometimes it can be hard to put your emotions into words, however. There is more to you than just being glad, sad, or mad. The list of feeling terms below can help you increase your emotional vocabulary. Of course, this list is just a start. There are several hundred emotion words in the English language, more than three hundred of which are in common use. The more your vocabulary grows, the better you will get at naming and expressing exactly what you're feeling.

Angst — anxiety about the future

Bliss — great happiness; spiritual joy

Confidence — being sure of yourself

Dread — great fear or anxiety

Elation — great joy or pride

Fury — violent anger

Grief — deep sadness from a loss

Hatred — extreme dislike; ill will

Irritability — being quick to get angry

Jumpiness — being nervous or jittery

Keenness — eagerness; enthusiasm

Loathing — great dislike and disgust

Melancholy — depression; a low mood

Numbness — being without emotion

Outrage — anger over an injury or insult

Panic — sudden, overpowering fright

Quarrelsomeness — being quick to argue

Remorse — distress caused by guilt

Smugness — annoyingly self-satisfied pride

Terror — extreme fear

Uneasiness — worry; social awkwardness

Vehemence — intense emotion

Wrath — strong, vengeful anger

Xenophobia — fear of anything foreign

Yearning — tender or urgent longing

Zest — keen enjoyment

definite time limit for the break. For example, you and a friend might agree to meet at lunch or after school to talk. Otherwise, it's tempting to keep putting off your discussion for so long that the problem never gets solved.

Use the energy. Once you've removed yourself from the situation, the risk of an argument may be over. However, you may still have upset feelings to handle. One way to do this is by channeling all that energy into doing something useful, such as exercising or cleaning your room.

Emotion in Motion

Some emotions are pleasant, and some are unpleasant, but all are good. This is because they all provide clues to how you are responding to the people and things around you. With practice, you can learn to decode these clues. You can then use this information to steer your thoughts and actions down the best path.

In general, unpleasant emotions are a sign that you believe something is wrong. For instance, you may feel angry if you think that someone has treated you unjustly. You may feel ashamed if you believe that you haven't lived up to your own standards. And you may be worried if you're convinced that something bad is going to happen.

In contrast, pleasant emotions are usually a sign that you believe things are going well. For instance, you may feel grateful if you think that someone has treated you kindly. You may be proud if you believe that you've met or exceeded your own standards. And you may be relieved if you conclude that nothing bad has occurred.

One emotion often leads to another in a chain reaction. For example, minor irritation that is left unchecked can turn into anger. Anger can turn into all-out rage. And rage is such a strong emotion that it can overwhelm your better judgment. This can lead to a hurtful remark or even physical violence. Afterward, you'll probably wind up feeling guilty. None of these is a very enjoyable emotion.

Fortunately, you have the power to break this chain. Your knowledge of what emotions mean and the bodily signs they cause can help you recognize anger early. This, in turn, gives you a chance to use cooling-off tactics. Once you've done that, you can figure out what the anger is telling you. This lets you find out what is wrong and look for ways to fix it. Abracadabra! You've just turned anger from a negative force into a positive one. That's the magic of understanding emotion.

Understanding Three Yourself

et's say you were watching TV when a newscaster announced a terrorism alert. There were rumors that terrorists might be planning to strike in your area. There was no proof that this was going to happen. Just to be on the safe side, though, people were being asked to be extra watchful for a few days.

How would you react to this situation? Would you turn off the news and start doing something else right away? Some people react to distressing news by trying to distract themselves. In our example, you might switch to another TV show, start playing a computer game, shoot a few baskets—anything to avoid thinking about the possible terrorist threat. If someone brought up the terrorism alert at school the next day, you would probably change the subject. This might make you feel better in the short run. In the long run, though, it could leave you feeling uneasy without understanding why.

At the other extreme, you could sit glued to the TV newscast for hours. Some people pay close attention to every detail of an upsetting situation. At times, however, they take this attention too far. In our example, you would probably be well aware of what you were feeling as you focused on the news. If you weren't careful, though, your worry could spiral out of control. You could wind up feeling swamped by a flood of anxiety.

Fortunately, there's a happy medium. Self-awareness is the act of paying attention to both your emotions and your thoughts about those emotions. You know what you're feeling, but you don't obsess about it. Instead, you are able to use your emotions in a positive way. In our example of the terrorism alert, you might realize that you were feeling a bit worried—a perfectly reasonable response. You would channel this energy into being extra alert for the next few days.

However, you wouldn't let the worry take over your life. You would be on the lookout for overly bleak thoughts. For example, let's say you caught yourself thinking, "Terrorists are going to strike! I'm in terrible danger. I have to keep watching the news." You could replace these thoughts with more real-istic ones: "Terrorists could strike, but they probably won't. I'm safe at home. Watching the news every minute won't change anything. All it will do is make me feel worse."

Underwhelming Emotion

Some people take lack of emotional self-awareness to an abnormal extreme. The scientific term for this is alexithymia. The term comes from the Greek a for "lack," lexis for "word," and thymos for "emotion." As the name implies, people with this problem lack the words to describe what they're feeling. In fact, they're almost totally unaware of their emotions. Not only are they out of touch with the helpful information that emotions can provide, but they also miss out on the other joys of a rich emotional life. Just as they aren't aware of fear, anger, or sadness, they also aren't aware of pleasure. In addition, they have few, if any, fantasies, and even their dreams tend to be dull. Eventually, people with alexithymia may realize they have trouble forming emotional bonds or enjoying their lives. Therapy can often help such people become more emotionally aware.

Your Own Personal Personality

Part of self-awareness is understanding how you naturally tend to respond to different situations. This is rooted in your temperament—your inborn tendency to react to events in a certain way. Your emotions change depending on what's going on around you. However, your temperament stays the same. It colors how you feel in any situation, which, in turn, affects how you think and behave.

Over time, your feelings, thoughts, and actions are likely to settle into a characteristic pattern. This pattern is your personality. It's your personal style of life and way of being. Each individual's personality is unique.

> *"What is it that distinguishes man from animal?... It is something altogether new, a previously unknown quality: self-awareness."*
> *—Erich Fromm (1900–1980),*
> *American psychologist*

Strictly speaking, personality isn't part of EI, but it's very closely related to it. Think of the difference this way: Your emotions are the way you feel *right now*. Your personality is the way you feel *most of the time*. Emotions may be fleeting, but personality lasts. It's a large part of what makes you who you are, day in and day out. Without EI, you wouldn't be aware of the habitual feelings that make up your personality. You wouldn't understand yourself very well. And you wouldn't be able to put your one-of-a-kind personality to the best use.

While no two people are identical, some individuals are more alike than others. For thousands of years, philosophers and psychologists have tried to group people into personality types based on their long-lasting traits. Around 400 B.C., the ancient Greek physician Hippocrates believed that people's health and personality could be traced to four fluids in the human body: blood, black bile, yellow bile, and phlegm. (Yellow bile is a fluid produced by the liver that aids digestion; and phlegm is the gloppy mucus that you sometimes cough up when you're sick. It's less clear what Hippocrates meant by black bile, but the name may have come from the dark color of dried blood.)

Hippocrates thought that the balance among these four fluids was critical. Too much blood made people sanguine, or cheerful. Too much black bile made them melancholic, or depressed. Too much yellow bile made them choleric, or irritable. And too much phlegm made them phlegmatic, or even-tempered.

Fast-forward to the 1920s. Swiss psychologist Carl Jung identified four basic psychological functions: thinking, feeling, sensing, and intuition. Jung saw thinking and feeling as judging functions, which means they are used to make decisions. He saw sensing (using the senses) and intuition (having hunches) as perceiving functions, which means they are used to gather information. Jung believed that everyone was stronger in one function than in the others. He also thought that people used this strongest function in a way that was either extraverted (more public) or introverted (more private).

"Who looks outside, dreams; who looks inside, awakes."
—Carl Jung (1875–1961),
Swiss psychologist

In the 1940s, Isabel Briggs Myers and her mother, Katharine Cook Briggs, were inspired by Jung's ideas. These two American women had no formal training in psychology. Yet they devised a personality test, called the Myers-Briggs Type Indicator, that is still widely used for career counseling. The test groups people into sixteen personality types based on their preferences for:

- extraversion or introversion
- sensing or intuition
- thinking or feeling
- judging or perceiving

This is only one system for classifying personality types. There are many others. No matter what system you use, however, the aim is increased understanding. The more you know about your own personality, in turn, the more self-accepting you're likely to become. You'll soon realize that there isn't one right or wrong way to be. Instead, there are just different styles that suit different people.

Building Your Confidence

The better you get to know yourself, the more confident you'll become. Confidence is faith in yourself and your abilities. This will surely grow as you become more aware of your personality strengths. Being confident doesn't mean you'll act annoyingly stuck-up. It just means that you won't be stalled by unrealistic self-doubts. When faced with a challenge, you won't feel helpless and hopeless. Instead, you'll feel ready to use your skills to rise to the occasion. Perhaps this is why Daniel Goleman, a leading figure in the EI field, considers self-confidence to be one of the core skills that make up EI.

Now is the time to become better acquainted with yourself. Start by asking yourself these questions: What are my major personality strengths and abilities? What are five things they've helped me accomplish? What are my weaknesses—the things I have trouble doing or haven't learned yet? What are five things I can do to change or make up for these weaknesses?

This kind of self-awareness can help you in all kinds of situations. Let's say you're thinking about going out for the

What's Your Type?

Exploring the Myers-Briggs system of personality types would create a book in itself. However, this quick test can give you a rough idea of what type you might be. First, answer four questions.

1. Which describes you better?
- extravert — focused on the outside world
- introvert — focused on your inner life

Write E (for Extravert) or I (for Introvert): _____

2. Which describes you better?
- sensing — focused on facts and reality
- intuitive — focused on hunches and possibilities

Write S (for Sensing) or N (for iNtuitive): _____

3. Which describes you better?
- thinking — make decisions based on logic
- feeling — make decisions based on values

Write T (for Thinking) or F (for Feeling): _____

4. Which describes you better?
- judging — prefer things to be planned out and settled
- perceiving — prefer things to be left open and flexible

Write J (for Judging) or P (for Perceiving): _____

Now, list the four letters in the same order as above:

_____ _____ _____ _____

This is the shorthand for your Myers-Briggs type. Following are some traits that people of specific types often have.

ENFJ — likes to focus on others; caring and concerned; good public speaker

ENFP — likes variety and challenge; lively and creative; good sense of humor

ENTJ — likes to be in charge; energetic and confident; enjoys a good debate

ENTP — likes variety and change; clever and creative; good problem-solver

ESFJ — likes to be needed; outgoing and warmhearted; good team player

ESFP — likes to talk; friendly and upbeat; generous with friends and family

ESTJ — likes being in charge; meets problems head-on; gets things done

ESTP — likes to always be on the go; confident and charming; strong sense of fun

INFJ — likes to work toward a vision; sensitive to others; keenly aware of emotions

INFP — likes pursuing own interests; dislikes rules and deadlines; strong inner values

INTJ — likes to come up with fresh ideas; original thinker; highly independent

INTP — likes to be precise and logical; quiet and self-reliant; deep thinker

ISFJ — likes to be helpful; loyal and dependable; pays attention to details

ISFP — likes to live and let live; easygoing and likable; enjoys simple pleasures

ISTJ — likes things to be orderly; reliable and responsible; good with facts and figures

ISTP — likes to stand back and observe; quiet and curious; highly independent soccer team. You haven't played much soccer before. However, you know that you're the kind of person who will show up for practices and try your hardest. You're good at working with other people. You like making new friends, and you're a fast runner. Knowing that you have so many things in your favor helps give you the confidence to try something new.

More About Me

Learn more about yourself by completing the following sentences.

One thing that makes me happy is _____.

I feel proud when _____.

I have faith in my ability to _____.

One thing that makes me angry is _____.

I feel sad when _____.

I get frustrated when I try to _____.

Ultimately, self-awareness teaches you not only about yourself, but also about other people. Let's say you join the soccer team, but you have trouble getting along with one of your teammates. You give it your all at every practice. Your teammate takes a more laid-back approach. Thanks to your knowledge of personality types, you realize that neither style is right or wrong. You and your teammate just have a different outlook on life, and that's actually a very good thing.

Working together on the same team can help you both stay balanced. Your teammate's more relaxed style helps keep you from being too hard on yourself. Your hardworking style helps keep your teammate from slacking off. This kind of give-and-take is a win-win situation. It is part of every good relationship, and it's where true understanding between people begins.

Handling Your Emotions

Remember the story about Josh and Becca that opened this book? Josh became upset after getting a D on a history test. He angrily blamed the teacher—even though he had gone to a movie the night before the test instead of studying. This didn't make sense to his friend Becca. Yet where strong emotions are involved, it's easy to let feelings overpower thinking. Chances are that you sometimes act unreasonably, too, when disappointed, hurt, or scared.

Take Josh's situation. Most likely, anger wasn't the first thing he felt. In fact, anger often arises in response to some other feeling that comes first. In this case, we can guess that what Josh felt first might have been regret that he hadn't studied. It might have been embarrassment that he got a lower grade than his friend. It might have been worry about how his mother would react when she found out about the grade. Or it could have been a complex mix of all these feelings.

As Josh grew more upset, however, these feelings gave way to anger. Josh's thoughts probably played a big role in the change. He may have started out by thinking, "I should have studied more." However, this may have been quickly followed by less reasonable thoughts: "It's pointless anyway. I'm just stupid. The teacher hates me. That test was totally unfair." Before long, Josh could have worked himself into a rage.

Things didn't have to turn out this way, though. By taking charge of his thoughts, Josh could have cut off this whole process before it got out of hand. As soon as he caught himself thinking, "It's pointless anyway. I'm just stupid," he could have stopped right there. Then he could have replaced these falsely negative thoughts with more accurately positive ones: "I'm not stupid. I just wasn't prepared for the test. Next time, I'll study more. I'll do better on the next test."

With his thoughts redirected this way, Josh's regret would have turned into determination to study and hopefulness about the next test. These emotions are the basis for motivation and optimism. And these attitudes, in turn, are the links that connect EI to success in life.

Too Much of a Good Thing

When people talk about keeping their emotions under control, they're usually referring to unpleasant feelings, such as anger or fear. However, even pleasant feelings need to be managed. Too much enthusiasm can lead to acting before you think. For example, you might be so excited about spending time after school with your friends that you sign up for band and choir and drama—then find that you've bitten off more than you can chew. Likewise, you might be so proud of an achievement that you brag about it to the point of annoying your friends. You can use the techniques in this chapter to handle positive feelings as well as negative ones.

Motivated to Move

What do Olympic athletes, world-class musicians, and U.S. presidents have in common? They're all extremely motivated to set goals and then work toward them. Motivation refers to the drive to pursue a goal. On a more modest scale, it can make the difference in winning a swim meet, excelling in band, or being voted class president. According to author and psychologist Daniel Goleman, motivation is one of the key parts of EI.

The word *motivation* comes from the Latin *movere*, for "to move." You may recall that this is also the source of the word *emotion*. Both motivation and emotion are forces that can propel you into action. They also feed off each other. Emotions such as confidence, pride, and even fear fuel motivated thoughts. These thoughts lead to the kind of behavior that moves you toward your goals. And this behavior often leads to the type of outcome that breeds more confidence and pride. This helpful cycle of emotion, thought, and behavior is at the core of EI.

The Three Main Parts of EI

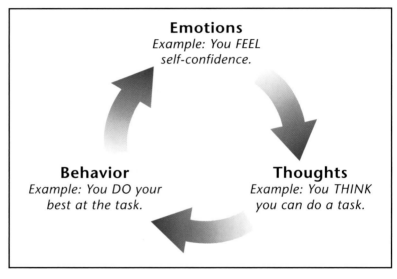

Emotions
Example: You FEEL self-confidence.

Thoughts
Example: You THINK you can do a task.

Behavior
Example: You DO your best at the task.

A helpful cycle that leads to positive results.

Let's say you have a book report due tomorrow. You know that you need to work on it, but you can't seem to get started. Instead, you talk to your friend on the phone for a while. Then you watch some TV. When you finally sit down in front of your computer, you wind up playing a game. Before long, two hours have passed, and you still haven't written one sentence. You're like a bike that is stuck in a rut—your wheels are spinning, but you're not going anywhere.

You can use your emotions to get out of this rut. First, ask yourself how you're feeling right now. Worried? Guilty? Afraid of failing the class if you don't finish the report? Next, close your eyes for a few minutes and imagine yourself turning in a great report tomorrow. Now how do you feel? Proud? Relieved? You can use this emotional energy to give yourself a pep talk. You might try thoughts such as these: "I've written lots of reports before. I know I can do this. I've read the book, and I'm well prepared to do a good job on the report."

"Thought is deeper than all speech, feeling deeper than all thought."
—Christopher Pearse Cranch
(1813–1892), American poet

You can use these thoughts, in turn, to redirect your energy toward writing. If your mind starts to wander, remind yourself, "I know I can write a good report. I just need to focus. It will feel great to have the report behind me." Once the report is completed, you'll probably feel exactly the way you imagined: proud and relieved. You'll have come full circle, and you'll wind up feeling good about yourself and the result.

Going for the Goal

Think of motivation as a car that drives you from point A to point B. You know where point A is, because that's where you are right now. But do you know where point B is? Until you've figured that out, you're just driving around aimlessly. That's why it is so important to learn to set goals. A goal is an end result toward which you direct your effort. In other words, it's the destination you want to reach through motivation and work. There are five parts to a SMART goal.

Specific — Goals should be narrow and clear. "Become a famous musician" is too broad. "Play my favorite song on the guitar" is better.

Measurable — Goals should be expressed as a number or some other objective measure of success. In the above example, you would need to spell out how you'll measure success at playing the song. For instance, "Play my favorite song on the guitar with no more than four mistakes."

Action-oriented — Goals should state an action that needs to be taken to achieve the desired outcome. Ask yourself: Does the goal contain an action verb? For instance, the example goal contains the action verb *play*.

Realistic — Goals should be challenging but attainable. Ask yourself: Does the goal fall somewhere between ridiculously easy and impossibly hard? In the above example, the goal would be realistic if there is a good match between your ability as a musician and the difficulty of the song you want to play.

Time-limited — Goals should have a definite deadline. Try to keep it less than a year away. For instance, the final wording of the example goal might be: "Play my favorite song on the guitar with no more than four mistakes by the end of next month."

Of course, there will be some goals that take much longer than a year to achieve. You can break them up into chunks, however. For example, if your long-term goal is to become a reporter, your shorter-term goal might be: "Write at least four articles for the school newspaper by the end of the semester."

Looking on the Bright Side

One of the best motivation boosters is optimism—the belief that, in general, things will turn out well. Optimistic people tend to see life in the best possible light. Pessimistic people, in contrast, tend to see it in the worst. Put a glass that is 50 percent filled on the table. The optimist will see it as half full, and the pessimist will see it as half empty.

Martin Seligman, an American psychologist, has suggested that optimists differ from pessimists mainly in the way they view problems. Pessimists tend to see problems as long-lasting. Optimists see them as temporary setbacks. Pessimists believe that one bad event will undermine everything they do. Optimists believe that a bad event is the exception rather than the rule. Pessimists tend to view everything as being their fault. Optimists take responsibility for things that are under their control. However, they don't blame themselves for things they can't help.

Optimism comes more naturally for some people than for others. Most people can learn to be more optimistic in their thinking patterns, though. As in the example of Josh and Becca, the trick is to first notice unrealistically negative thoughts, then replace them with more realistically positive ones. This is harder than it sounds, however. Many negative thoughts are so fleeting that you're barely aware of them. Often, the same negative thoughts pop up again and again. Over time, this kind of thinking can become a habit. It takes real effort to watch for such thoughts and kick the habit of negative thinking.

Let's say you are a student who uses a wheelchair. Watching your classmates play sports, you get discouraged. If you always tell yourself, "I can't do anything," you'll just grow more down-hearted. However, if you notice this thought and think it over, you'll soon realize it's not true. There are many, many things you *can* do. You might replace your falsely negative thought with a more accurately positive one: "I can do lots of things. I'm really fast in this chair, and my arms are very strong." This kind of thinking, in turn, might motivate you to take positive action, such as joining a wheelchair basketball team.

Of course, you can't ignore reality. It would be pointless to tell yourself, "I can jump out of this wheelchair and run," if that's not true. The aim isn't to deceive yourself. Instead, it is to recast the situation in a more honest light. Given the way many people think, however, this often means turning negative thoughts into more positive ones.

The rewards of greater optimism are many. Studies have found that pessimists tend to give up more easily and become depressed more often than optimists. In contrast, optimists tend to do better at school, sports, and work. They may even enjoy better physical health. There is much to be said for learning to look at the bright side of life.

Managing Relationships

Picture this: Luis is walking home from school when three older boys block his path on the sidewalk. "Where do you think you're going?" the biggest one demands. Luis tries to ignore the question and go around the boys, but the big one pushes him. "Hey, you don't pass until I say you pass!" he growls. Luis wants to run, but he can't, because the other boys have circled around him. Besides, the other students walking home behind him might see. He's almost as scared of being embarrassed as he is of getting beaten up.

Luis has just encountered a bully—something that happens to most students at one time or another. Fortunately, Luis can use his EI skills to cope with this difficult situation. Right off the bat, Luis realizes that he's afraid. His heart is pounding, he's sweating, and his mind is a blur. He knows that he needs to calm down for two reasons: One, he needs to have his wits about him if he's going to think his way out of this situation, and two, bullies thrive on frightening people. If Luis openly shows his fear, he'll be giving the bullies exactly what they want.

Luis's fear is quickly turning into anger anyway. He thinks, "Who do these guys think they are? I'll show them. I could kick the big one in the shin before he even knows what's happening." Almost immediately, however, Luis realizes that this is a bad idea. Violence will only make things worse.

Luis takes a couple of long, deep breaths to relax his body and clear his mind. He tells himself, "These guys can't rattle me. I'm in charge of my own feelings. I'm feeling calmer already. I know how to handle myself." Luis squares his shoulders and stands tall. He looks the biggest guy straight in the eye. His body language says that he is confident and not vulnerable, because any sign of weakness will only encourage the bully. Then, Luis says in a firm, calm voice, "What's up? Hey, are you going to the game tonight?"

This isn't the reaction the bully had bargained for. He had expected Luis to shout, fight back, or maybe even cry. He hadn't expected friendly-sounding conversation. The bully seems surprised and confused. Luis seizes this moment of confusion to say, "Maybe I'll see you at the game. Later." Then he edges past the boys and makes his way up the sidewalk. Thanks to EI, then, Luis is able to recognize and handle his own fear and anger. He's also able to guess what is going on in the bully's mind and predict how the bully will behave. This gives him the edge in a sticky situation.

Bully-Busting Tips

Bullying can be physical (pushing, hitting, kicking, etc.) or verbal (name-calling, insults, racist remarks, etc.). If you're the target of this kind of behavior, it's not your fault. In fact, it reveals much more about the bully than it does about you. Bullies often are insecure, so they put other people down to make themselves feel powerful and important. Many are angry because they have themselves been the victims of abuse in the past. Instead of venting their anger at the abuser, though, they take it out on someone they see as weaker. The key to outsmarting most bullies is not to let them get a visible rise out of you. If you look scared or angry, it just feeds their need to wield power over you. On the other hand, if you act calm and unfazed, you take away their fun.

Reading Others Like a Book

In threatening situations, the ability to read other people is a survival skill. In less tense situations, it helps you get along with others and achieve your goals. Of course, the things people say about what they're feeling and thinking are important. However, many people aren't very aware of their own emotions and thoughts, and those who are may not always be honest about them. This is why it's helpful to look for other clues as well. Facial expressions are among the most reliable signs of what people are truly feeling.

Charles Darwin, the great British scientist who is best known for his theory of evolution, recognized this fact more than 130 years ago. In 1872, Darwin published a book called *The Expression of the Emotions in Man and Animals*. In this book, he described the facial expressions of not only humans, but also cats, dogs, horses, and other animals. Darwin believed that facial expressions of emotion had evolved over time. He thought they were inborn and universal. This meant that a smile or a frown should convey the same feeling to people all over the world.

At first, many people questioned Darwin's views. Even some noted scientists believed that all expressions were learned and that they varied from culture to culture, the way language does. Over the last forty years, however, these opposing views have been put to the test in scientific research. In general, the studies have supported Darwin's claims.

"The face is the mirror of the mind, and eyes without speaking confess the secrets of the heart."
—*St. Jerome (c. 342–420), Catholic scholar*

Paul Ekman, an American psychologist, is among the leading researchers in this field today. In an early study, he showed photographs of facial expressions to people from five countries: the United States, Chile, Argentina, Brazil, and Japan. He then asked the people to judge what emotion was being depicted in each photo. Most people agreed, no matter what country they were from.

Not everyone was convinced, however. It was always possible that people had learned what the expressions meant through contact with Americans or by seeing American TV, movies, and magazines. To prove that expressions were really inborn, Ekman would have to show that they were the same even in a culture where people were almost completely cut off from the outside world. He found such a culture among the native tribesmen in Papua, New Guinea. His studies there showed that Americans and New Guinea tribesmen agreed on what a happy, angry, disgusted, or sad face looks like. No matter where in the world you live, a smile means you're happy, a glare indicates anger, a wrinkled nose indicates

Face Facts

Humans seem to naturally understand many facial expressions. However, you can learn to get even better at reading faces with regular practice. Honing this skill takes effort. It isn't always easy to pick out the subtle differences between an angry face and a frightened one, for example. Following are some signs to watch for.

Anger
- inner corners of the eyebrows pulled down and together
- eyes opened wide
- lips narrowed and sometimes pressed tightly together

Disgust
- nose scrunched up
- upper lip curled up

Fear
- eyebrows raised and drawn together
- eyes opened wide

Happiness
- lips drawn into a smile
- cheeks pushed up
- eyes squeezed together slightly to form crow's-feet wrinkles

Sadness
- inner corners of the eyebrows pulled up and together
- vertical crease between the eyebrows
- corners of the mouth turned down

Surprise
- eyebrows raised but not drawn together
- mouth opened with jaw dropped

As you start paying more attention to facial expressions, you may be amazed by how many variations you see. According to Ekman, the muscles in the human face are capable of making more than 10,000 different expressions! The expressions shown on these two pages seem to be especially helpful for identifying emotions, though. The more you practice, the better you'll get at recognizing these key expressions.

disgust, and a frown means you're sad. It's a universal language that anyone can understand.

Reading Between the Lines

There are other clues to what someone else may be feeling. These include the same signs of bodily arousal that you notice in yourself. When people start to breathe faster for no obvious reason, they may be feeling almost any kind of strong emotion. When they suddenly begin to sweat, they may be afraid. When their face turns red, they may be embarrassed, angry, ashamed, or guilty. When their face turns white, they may be afraid or angry.

Someone's tone of voice can reveal a lot, too. People who are angry, afraid, or excited often start talking louder and faster. In the case of anger or fear, the pitch of their voice may also be raised. On the other hand, those who are sad or bored may talk softer and slower. In the case of sadness, the pitch of their voice may also be lowered.

Then there is body language. When people stand up straight and tall, they're sending a message that they're confident and determined. When they lean toward you while you're talking, they're showing their interest. When they fidget and tap their fingers, they're showing just the opposite. And when they look you straight in the eyes, they're more than likely being honest.

To see how much information you can glean from facial expressions and body language alone, try this experiment: Watch a TV drama or comedy for a few minutes with the sound on mute. Try to guess which emotions are being portrayed based on people's faces and gestures alone. Then turn on the sound and see how accurate your guesses were. Chances are that you will be able to figure out some things people are feeling without hearing a single word they are saying.

Can't people learn to fake some of these signals? Of course. However, it would be very hard to fake all of them at once. Let's say you find a fresh stain on your favorite T-shirt, even though you haven't worn it lately. You suspect that your sister wore the shirt without asking and accidentally stained it. When you ask her about it, she looks you straight in the eye and denies it. At the same time, though, her face turns red. You conclude that she may be feeling guilty.

That might be true. On the other hand, your sister could be turning red simply because she's angry that you don't trust her. Learning to read people's emotions isn't as straightforward as reading this book. It's more like solving a complex mystery. Usually, there is no single piece of information that tells the whole story. Instead, it's a matter of putting together all the clues and looking for the most likely explanation.

Lie Detectors

Spotting a lie takes practice. These are some of the signs that clever detectives, attorneys, teachers, and parents watch for. Keep in mind that these signs don't necessarily prove that the other person is lying. However, they may tip you off to be a little more cautious about taking what the person says at face value.

- *not looking you in the eye*
- *fidgeting*
- *shifting back and forth*
- *change in tone of voice*
- *talking fast*
- *sweating*
- *blinking the eyes a lot*
- *licking the lips*
- *turning red*
- *any sign of an emotion that doesn't fit what the person is saying*

Stopping Fights Before They Start

Once you know how to read other people, you can use that information to head off many arguments. Of course, people will always have different views about some things. It's okay if people share those differing opinions. In fact, that's how people learn from one another. However, there are helpful ways to share, and there are unhelpful ways. Take the wrong approach, and an interesting debate can quickly turn into an angry argument. This may be why author and psychologist Daniel Goleman considers conflict management to be another of the core skills that make up EI.

Fortunately, EI gives you the skills you need to manage conflict in a positive way. For one thing, it helps you spot any angry feelings that may be brewing, either in yourself or in other people. Once you recognize these feelings, you can take steps to calm things down. For example, you might try making a joke to lighten up the situation.

EI also gives you tools for resolving disputes in a group. For example, you might try asking for help to find a solution. This approach gets people thinking of ways to work together rather than against one another. Or you could compromise, offering to give up part of what you want in order to get the rest of it.

To sum up, here are some useful strategies for avoiding or resolving conflicts.

Defusing anger

- using humor—looking at things in a lighthearted way to ease the tension
- postponing—putting off discussion until everyone is calmer
- expressing regret—saying you are sorry about something without taking blame

Resolving disputes

- requesting help—asking people to work with you to find a joint solution
- taking turns—giving each person an equal chance to speak or do things
- sharing—cooperating with others to use resources or do a task together
- problem-solving—brainstorming as a group to come up with possible solutions
- compromising—giving up part of what you want in order to get the rest of it
- seeking mediation—asking people who aren't involved to resolve a dispute

"The key to making...relationships and interactions successful so that they benefit all concerned—not the least, you—is emotional intelligence."
—Hendrie Weisinger,
American psychologist

"I Feel Your Pain"

EI is very helpful when you need to resolve problems with other people. However, it also comes in handy when you simply want to make friends and get along. One of the best things about EI is that it helps you develop greater empathy—an insightful awareness of the feelings, thoughts, and experiences of another person. Although empathy and sympathy sound alike, they're actually different things. Let's say your friend's parents have just gotten a divorce. Sympathy means you feel sorry for her. Empathy means you mentally put yourself in her place. You understand what she must be going through, and you grasp the meaning of her feelings and behavior.

If you understand where someone is coming from, it makes it easier to guess where that person is going. In other words, empathy makes it easier to predict what someone's next move will be. This, in turn, gives you a chance to steer the situation in a helpful direction. Think back to the story about the bully at the beginning of this chapter. If Luis hadn't been able to anticipate the bully's reaction, he might have shown more fear or lashed out angrily. These actions probably would have just set the bully off, and the outcome might have been explosive.

If you know what makes people tick, their differences also seem less strange and more understandable. Therefore, empathy makes it possible to feel respect for someone who has a different viewpoint from your own. Think about a time when you worked with other students in a group. Chances are that things went well if there was a lot of friendly give-and-take among the students. On the other hand, if there was a lot of fighting about whose ideas were "right" and whose were "wrong," the group may have spent so much time bickering that little else was accomplished.

Listen Up!

A big part of empathy is being a good listener. When someone is talking to you, it helps to show that you're paying attention if you look into the speaker's eyes. You can also nod or say "Uh-huh" now and then. Try not to fidget or interrupt. If you don't understand something, wait for a pause. Then say, "I want to make sure I under-stand. What do you mean by...?" Even if you think you understand, it's a good idea to double-check this. When the speaker pauses, restate what he or she has just said in your own words. For example, you might say, "I think you're saying that..." or "You sound like you're feeling..." If you've got it wrong, this gives the speaker a chance to clear things up. If you've got it right, the speaker now knows that you're in sync.

Finally, if you know how people are apt to respond, it helps you communicate more effectively with them. Let's say you have a friend who always cracks jokes about your skinny legs. You could say, "You're such a jerk!" Trading insults will only make things worse, however. On the other hand, you could use your EI and say, "When you make a crack like that, I feel embarrassed. I know you don't mean it to hurt my feelings, but it does." You've let the other person know that you think he's a basically a nice guy. At the same time, though, you've clearly explained what bothers you and why. This approach is much more likely to get the response you want.

In almost any situation, EI makes it easier for you to achieve your goals, whatever they may be. EI gives you the skills you need to:

- handle other people's emotions in a positive way
- be aware of other people's emotions
- use emotions to improve your thinking
- handle your own emotions in a positive way
- be aware of your own emotions
- know about emotions and their meanings

In short, EI is useful in every aspect of your life. It helps you get along with others and be more sensitive to their feelings. It gives you motivation to pursue your goals. It helps you find effective ways to cope with unpleasant emotions. And it puts you in touch with your own fascinating feelings.

Glossary

- **alexithymia:** a disorder in which people are almost totally unaware of their emotions

- **arousal:** the bodily changes that go along with emotional states

- **dysphoria:** an unpleasant mood

- **emotion:** a mental feeling that arises without conscious effort and leads to a state of arousal

- **emotional intelligence (EI):** the ability to notice, understand, and manage your own emotions and those of others; this lets you use emotional information to guide your thoughts and actions in a helpful way empathy: an insightful awareness of the feelings, thoughts, and experiences of another person

euphoria: an overly keyed-up mood

euthymia: a mood that leads to mental peace and happiness

goal: an end result toward which you direct your effort

intelligence: the ability to learn and then put that learning to good use

interpersonal intelligence: the ability to understand the feelings and goals of other people

intrapersonal intelligence: the ability to understand your own feelings and goals

mood: a mental feeling that is longer-lasting and wider-ranging than an emotion

motivation: the drive to pursue a goal

optimism: the belief that, in general, things will turn out well personality: a characteristic pattern of feeling, thinking, and behaving

practical intelligence: the ability to understand and solve real-life problems

repression: the forcing of unpleasant feelings or painful memories from the conscious part of the mind to the unconscious

self-awareness: the act of paying attention to both your emotions and your thoughts about those emotions

temperament: the inborn tendency to react to events in a certain way

Further Resources

Books

Andrews, Linda Wasmer. *Intelligence*. Danbury, Conn.: Franklin Watts, 2003.
This book discusses various types of intelligence, including EI.

Baron, Renee. *What Type Am I? Discover Who You Really Are.* New York: Penguin Books, 1998.
This book about the Myers-Briggs Type Indicator is written for adults, but older teens will find it fascinating as well.

Delis-Abrams, Alexandra. *The Feelings Dictionary*. Coeur d'Alene, Idaho: ABC Feelings, 1999.
This dictionary contains simple definitions for a few hundred feeling terms, from *abandoned* to *zonked*.

Egeberg, Gary. *My Feelings Are Like Wild Animals! How Do I Tame Them?* Mahwah, N.J.: Paulist Press, 1998.
This book, geared toward Christian teens, is a guide to handling unpleasant emotions.

Espeland, Pamela. *Knowing Me, Knowing You: The I-Sight Way to Understand Yourself and Others*. Minneapolis: Free Spirit, 2001.
This book offers another way of exploring your personality type and building self-awareness.

Kaufman, Gershen, Lev Raphael, and Pamela Espeland. *Stick Up for Yourself! Every Kid's Guide to Personal Power and Positive Self-Esteem*. Minneapolis: Free Spirit, 1999.
This book is filled with great advice on handling your feelings and dealing with other people.

Kincher, Jonni. *Psychology for Kids: 40 Fun Tests That Help You Learn About Yourself*. Minneapolis: Free Spirit, 1995.
This book is filled with fun activities that help you learn more about your feelings, attitudes, and behavior.

Kincher, Jonni. *Psychology for Kids II: 40 Fun Experiments That Help You Learn About Others*. Minneapolis: Free Spirit, 1995.
This book is similar to the one above except that the activities help you learn more about other people.

Seaward, Brian Luke, with Linda K. Bartlett. *Hot Stones and Funny Bones: Teens Helping Teens Cope with Stress and Anger.* Deerfield Beach, FL.: Health Communications, Inc., 2002.
This book is packed with helpful suggestions for dealing with stress and anger.

Silverman, Robin L. *Reaching Your Goals.* Danbury, Conn.: Franklin Watts, 2004.
This book examines how to use imagination, thought, determination, and visualization to transform wishes into goals.

Stacy, Lori. *Discover Yourself! The Official All About You Book of Quizzes.* New York: Scholastic, 2000.
This book for girls has twenty-five fun quizzes to help you learn more about your personality, relationships, and interests.

Youngs, Bettie B., and Jennifer Leigh Youngs. *A Taste-Berry Teen's Guide to Setting and Achieving Goals.* Deerfield Beach, FL: Health Communications, Inc., 2002.
This book, geared toward older teens, has tips on motivation and goal-setting.

Online Sites and Organizations

American Psychological Association

www.apa.org

This site provides information about the science of emotion and behavior.

Consortium for Research on Emotional Intelligence in Organizations

www.eiconsortium.org

The scientists in this group study and use Daniel Goleman's model of EI.

Six Seconds Emotional Intelligence Network

www.6seconds.org

This site, run by a nonprofit group, describes some interesting ways in which schools are helping students to develop their EI skills.

Index

About the Author

Linda Wasmer Andrews is a freelance writer from Albuquerque, New Mexico. She specializes in writing about psychology and health. Linda is the author of seven earlier books, including *Intelligence* and *Meditation*. She also has written more than 1,700 articles for magazines, newsletters, and websites. Linda firmly believes that talent and hard work are only half of what it takes to be successful at writing (or at anything else, for that matter). Emotional intelligence is the other half. In addition to writing full-time, Linda recently completed a master's degree in health psychology from Capella University.

Acknowledgments
Many thanks to Hendrie Weisinger, Ph.D.,
psychologist, author, and EI guru.